Amazing Webs

Written by Clare Helen Welsh

Collins

Spiders are all around us, but don't be afraid. Spiders have amazing web-spinning skills.

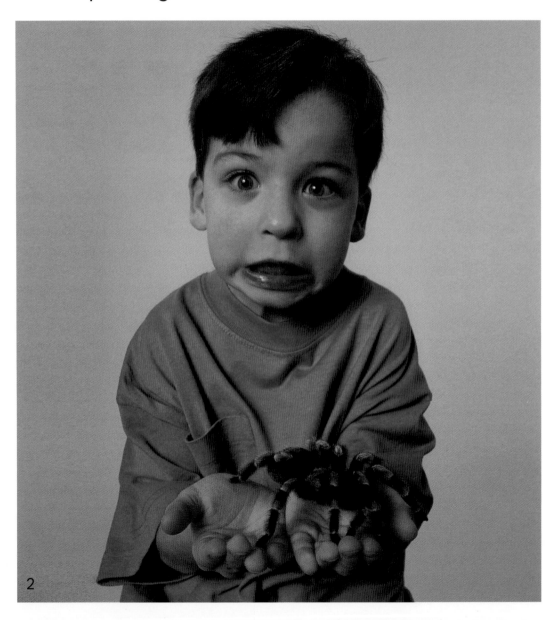

Webs are complex
forms made from
a spider's silk.

Most spiders spin fine silk from spinneret glands near their abdomen.

abdomen

spinnerets

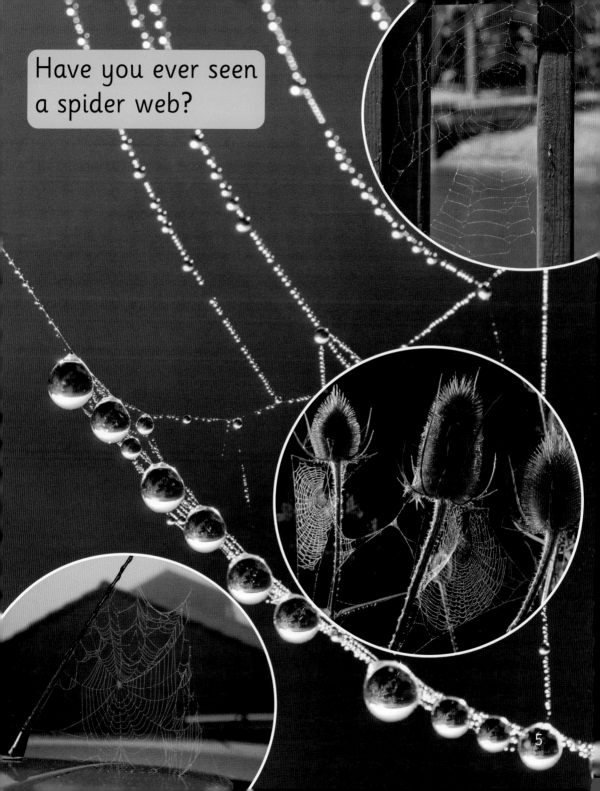

Have you ever seen a spider web?

5

Spider silk is thinner than human hair.
For its size, it is stronger than steel!

spider silk under a microscope

Spider silk can be made into fabric. Look at this spider silk vest!

Spiders make webs to trap and eat insects.

Spiders use their silk to get around too!

Spiders sometimes decorate their webs with extra bits of silk. This might be to attract insects.

This web belongs to the golden orb spider.
It is made from spokes and ring shapes.

spokes

Some webs protect spiders' eggs.

The brown recluse spider encases its eggs in a web-like sac.

sac

Some webs, like this one, are found on the ground.

funnel web

hobo spider

Sheet webs are made between twigs and trees.

sheet web

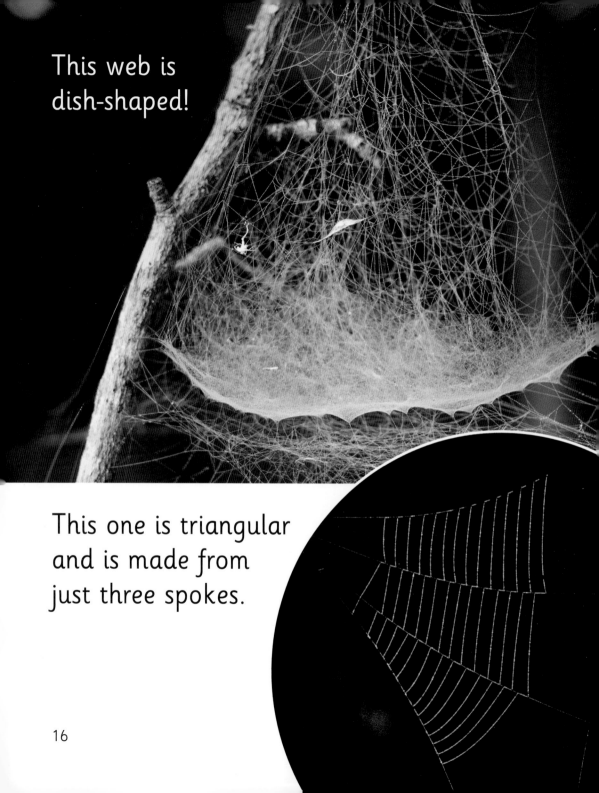

This web is dish-shaped!

This one is triangular and is made from just three spokes.

16

This is a house spider.
It makes cobwebs.

A cobweb is
an irregular kind
of spider web.

cobweb

Not all spiders make webs. These spiders hunt for their food.

jumping spider

fishing spider

tarantula

crab spider

19

Spiders are important in the food chain.
They are a fine snack for birds!

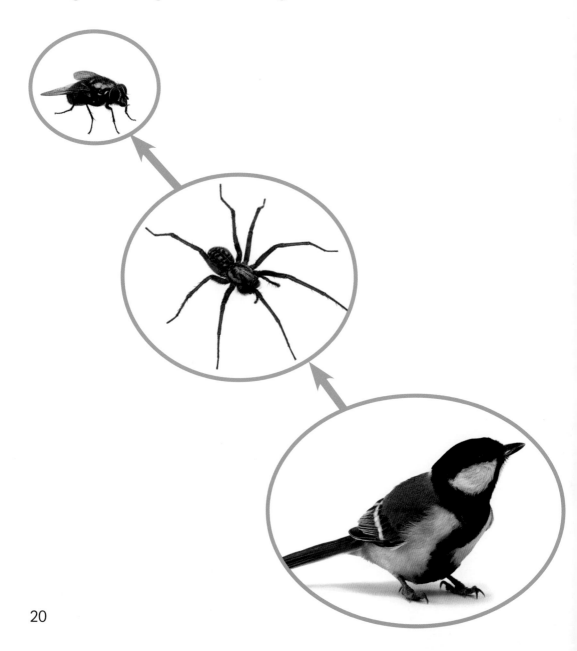

They help people too. Their amazing webs trap irritating insects in our homes.

Amazing webs

🐾 Review: After reading 🐾

Use your assessment from hearing the children read to choose any GPCs, words or tricky words that need additional practice.

Read 1: Decoding

- Turn to page 17 and point to **irregular**. Discuss how we can check its meaning (not even/clear in shape) by comparing the cobwebs with the more evenly shaped spider web on page 16.
- Ask the children to read these words. Ask: Which word does not contain either an /oa/ or an /igh/ sound? (*house*)
  don't   most   protect   kind   house   triangular   spokes   spiders   fine
- Point to labels for the children to read out loud. Say: Can you blend in your head as you read these words?

Read 2: Prosody

- Discuss how we can use emphasis when reading to make connections.
- Model reading page 18, emphasising **Not all** and **These**. Explain how this makes it clear that by "these" we mean the spiders that don't make webs.
- Ask the children to read pages 18 and 19, using emphasis as above, and for the different spider names (**jumping**, **fishing**, **tarantula**, **crab**).

Read 3: Comprehension

- Ask: What spider webs have you seen? What did they look like? Were they similar/ different to these?
- Return to the front cover. Ask: Why do you think the author chose this title? Focus on the word **Amazing**. Ask: Do you think the webs are amazing? Why?
- Ask the children the following questions which are focused on finding and comparing information:
  - What's the quickest way you can find the page on jumping spiders? (*look through the pages at the labels*)
  - Reread page 18 and ask: What do these names of spiders have in common? (e.g. *they show how they move*)
  - On page 20, ask: Why are the bird and fly in the same diagram? (*they are both in the same food chain*) What does the spider eat in the food chain? (*fly*)
- Turn to pages 22–23 and ask the children to tell you what they can recall about the different types of webs that spiders make. Ask: Have you ever seen any of these spider webs?